THE QUEEN'S GAMBIT

MUSIC FROM THE NETFLIX LIMITED SERIES
MUSIC BY CARLOS RAFAEL RIVERA

Additional Music by David Stal and Asuka Ito

Arranged and edited for piano by Kait Dunton

ISBN 978-1-70516-335-1

Visit Hal Leonard Online at
www.halleonard.com

World headquarters, contact:
Hal Leonard
7777 West Bluemound Road
Milwaukee, WI 53213
Email: info@halleonard.com

In Europe, contact:
Hal Leonard Europe Limited
1 Red Place
London, W1K 6PL
Email: info@halleonardeurope.com

In Australia, contact:
Hal Leonard Australia Pty. Ltd.
4 Lentara Court
Cheltenham, Victoria, 3192 Australia
Email: info@halleonard.com.au

MAIN TITLE

Music by
CARLOS RAFAEL RIVERA

Moderately fast, in 2 ♩. = 120

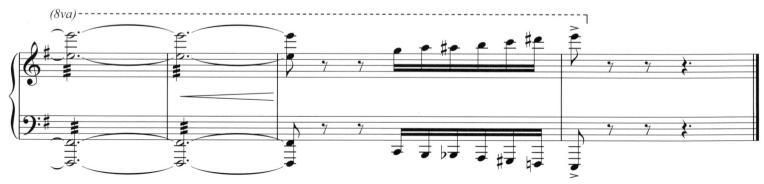

PLAYING TOWNES

Music by CARLOS RAFAEL RIVERA
and DAVID STAL

Moderately, in 3 ♩. = 76

Pedal ad lib. throughout

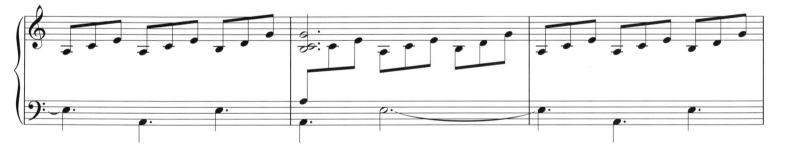

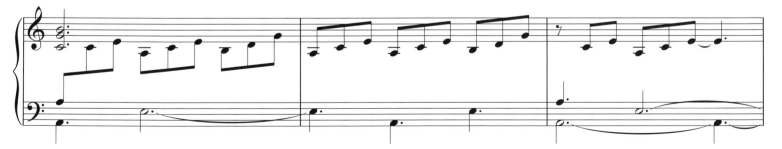

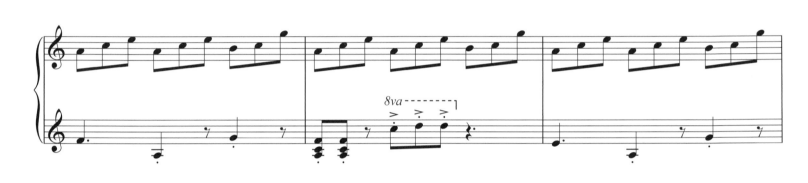

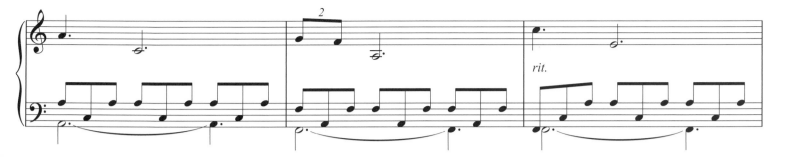

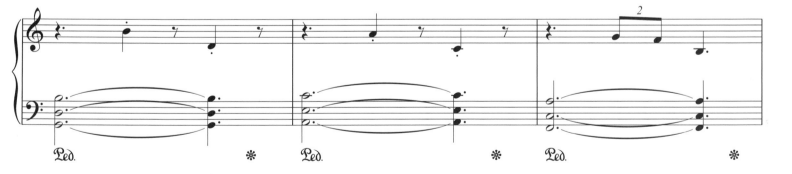

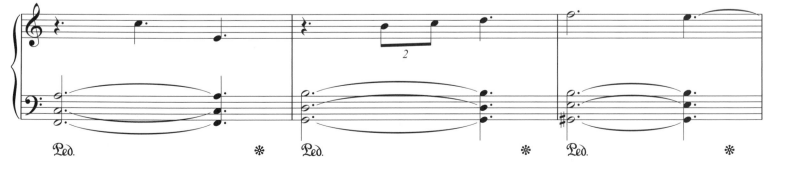

Ped.   ✳

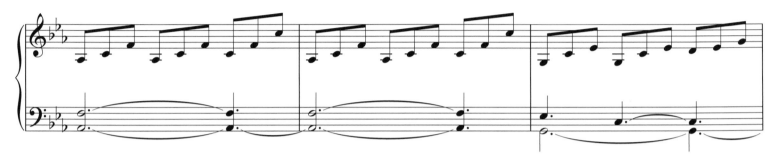

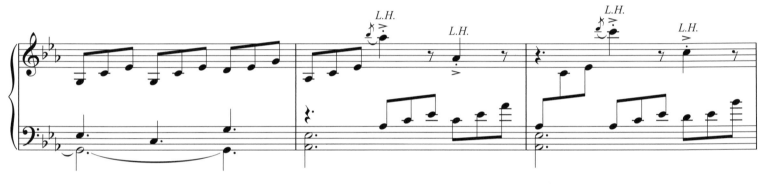

Slightly Faster

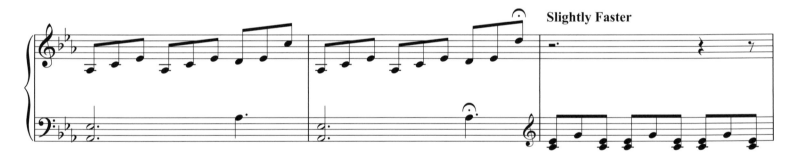

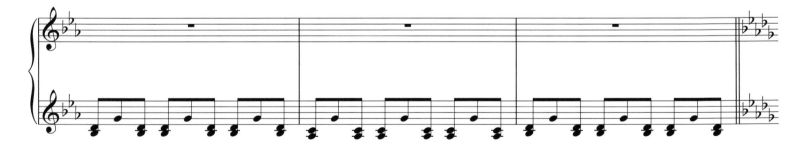

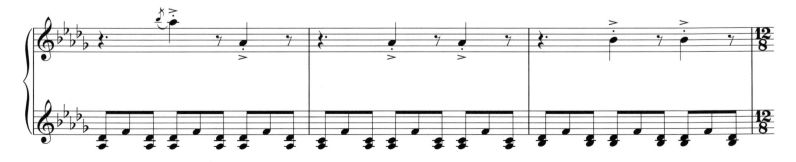

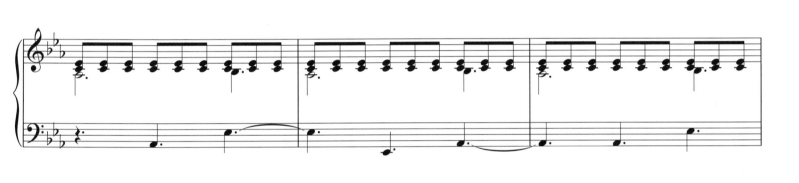

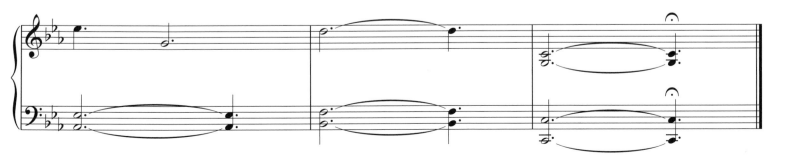

BETH'S STORY

Music by
CARLOS RAFAEL RIVERA

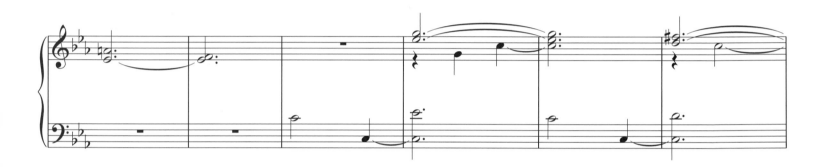

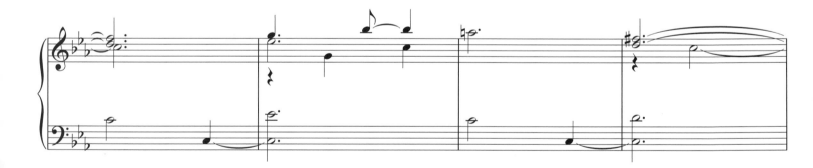

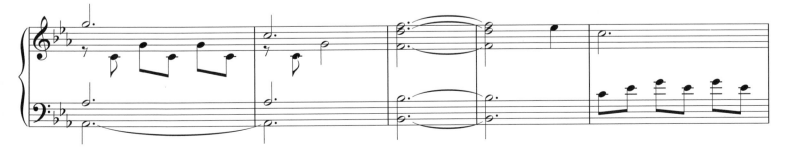

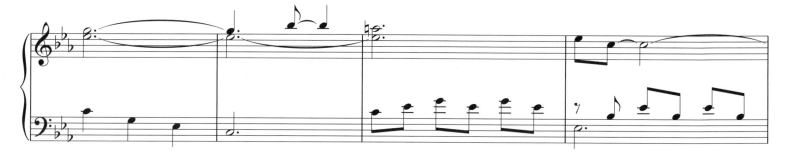

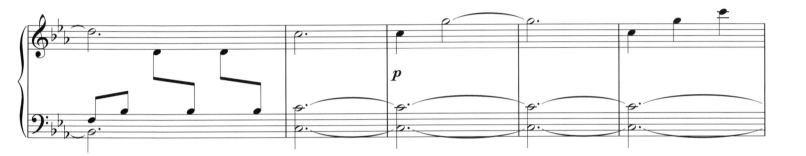

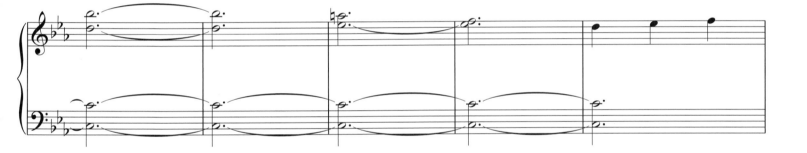

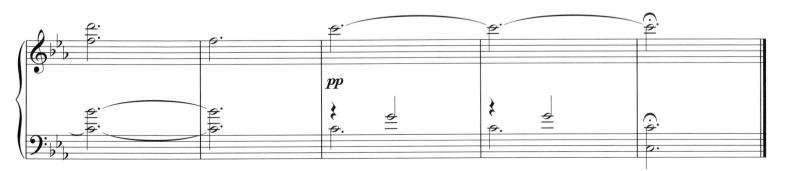

METHUEN HOME FOR CHILDREN 1957

Music by
CARLOS RAFAEL RIVERA

Moderately ♩ = 96

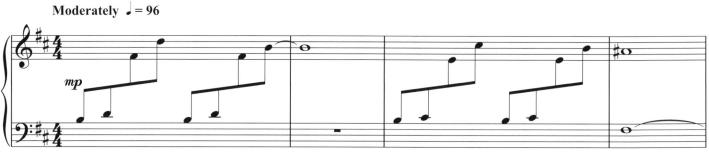

Pedal ad lib. throughout

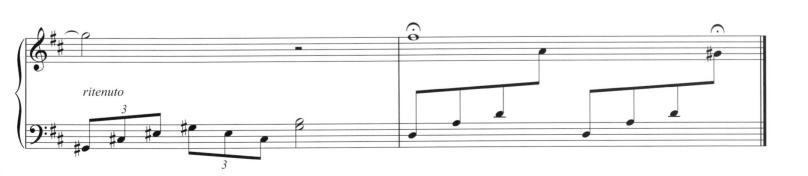

YOU'RE GLOATING

Music by
CARLOS RAFAEL RIVERA

Moderately fast ♩ = 135

mp

Pedal ad lib. throughout

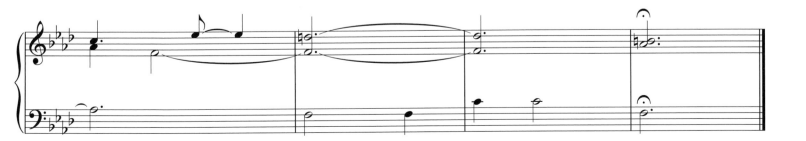

TRAINING WITH MR. SCHAIBEL

Music by CARLOS RAFAEL RIVERA
and ASUKA ITO

Moderately ♩ = 108

Pedal ad lib. throughout

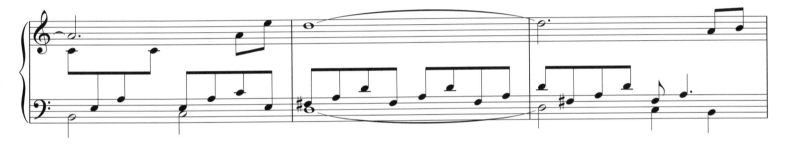

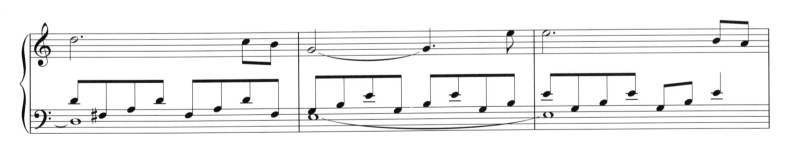

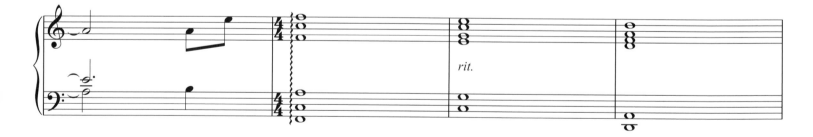

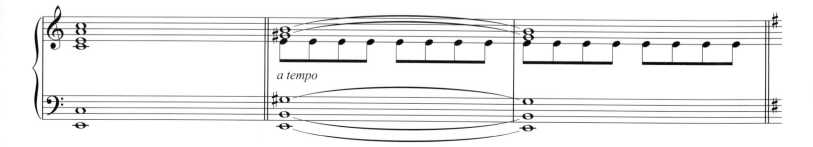

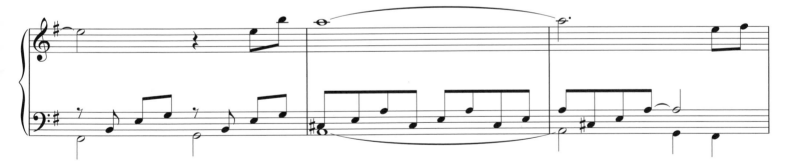

CEILING GAMES

Music by CARLOS RAFAFEL RIVERA
and ASUKA ITO

Moderately fast ♩ = 120

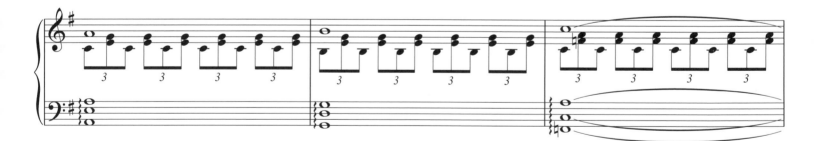

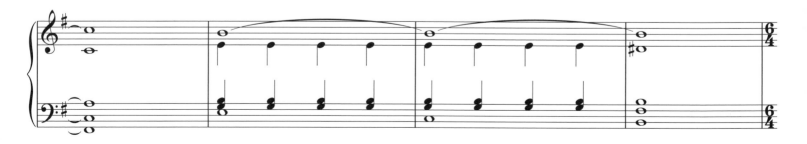

BETH ALONE

Music by CARLOS RAFAEL RIVERA
and LUKAS FRANK

Moderately ♩ = 100

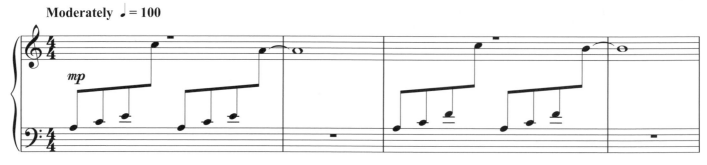

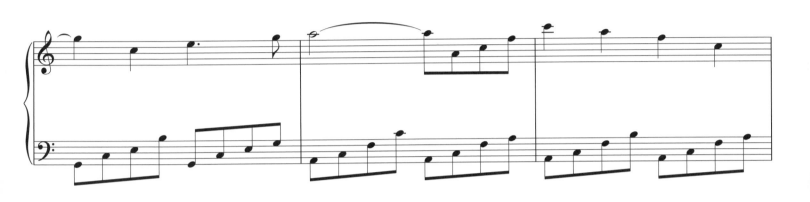

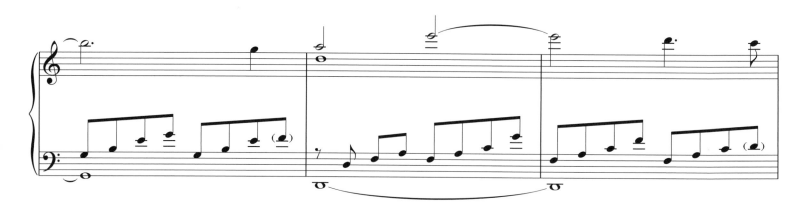

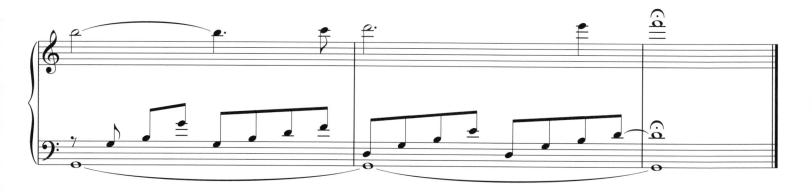

OHIO US CHAMPIONSHIP 1967

Music by CARLOS RAFAEL RIVERA
and ASUKA ITO

Moderately ♩ = 84

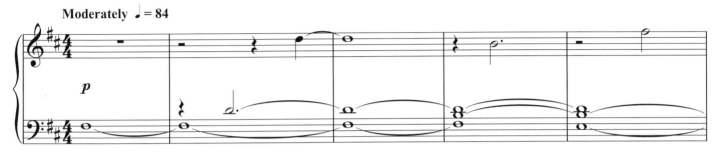

JOLENE!

Music by
CARLOS RAFAEL RIVERA

Moderately, in 1 ♩ = 156

Pedal ad lib. throughout

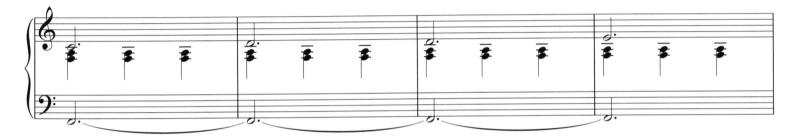

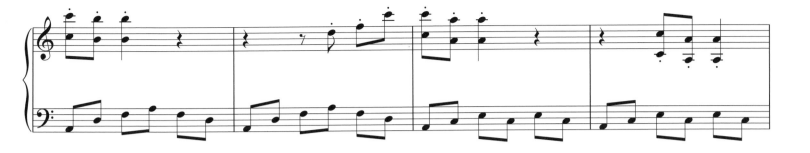

MOSCOW INVITATIONAL 1968

Music by CARLOS RAFAEL RIVERA
and DAVID STAL

Moderately ♩ = 144

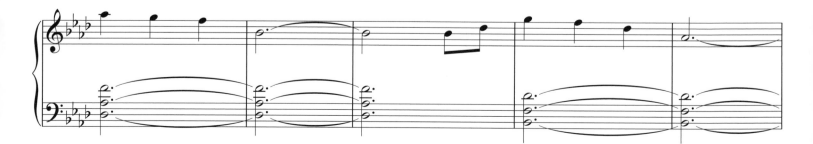

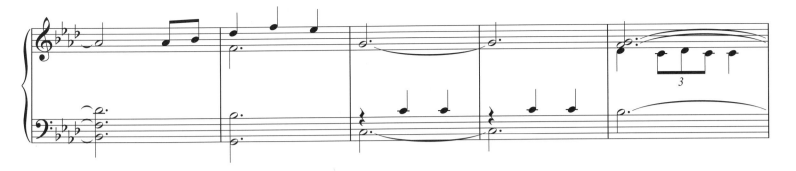

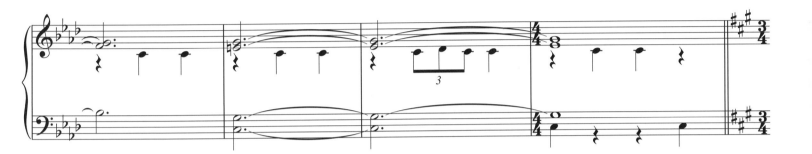

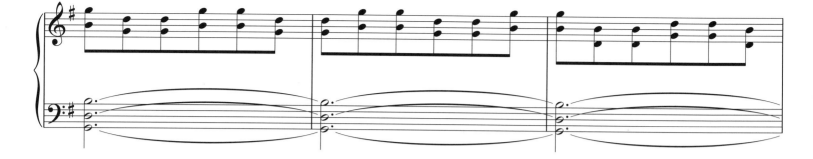

THE FINAL GAME

Music by
CARLOS RAFAEL RIVERA

Moderately slow, in 1 ♩ = 144

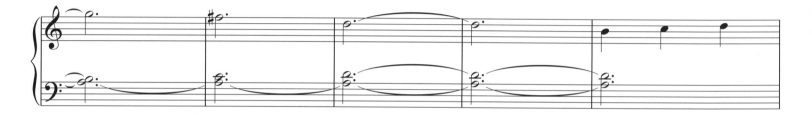

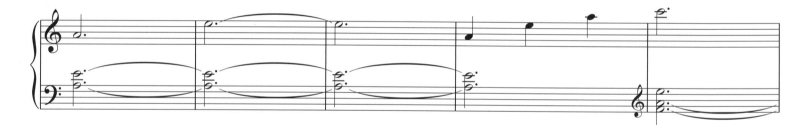

♩ = 100

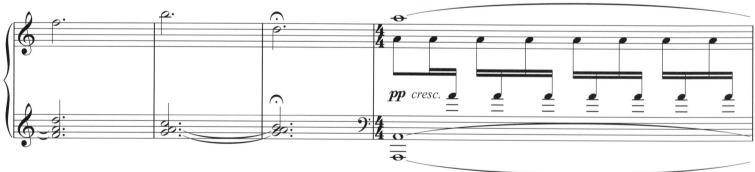

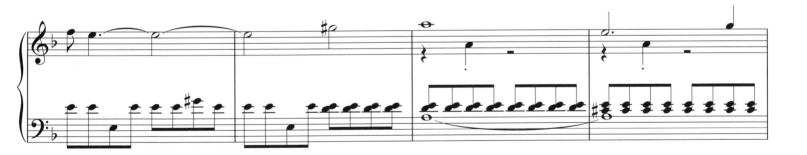

TAKE IT, IT'S YOURS

Music by
CARLOS RAFAEL RIVERA

Moderately, in 2 ♩. = 80

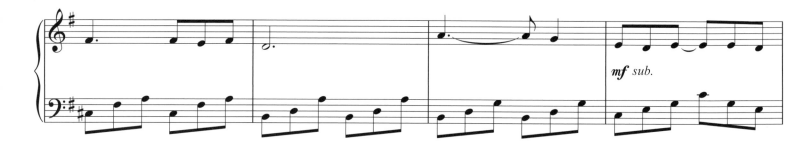

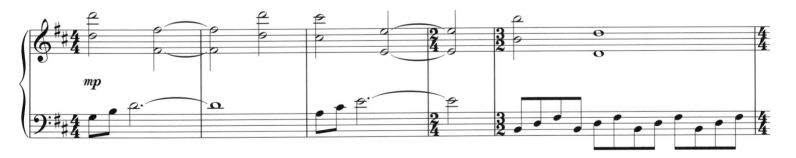

SYGRAYEM
(Let's Play)

Music by
CARLOS RAFAEL RIVERA

Moderately, steadily ♩ = 112

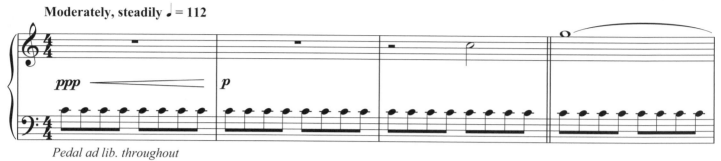

Pedal ad lib. throughout

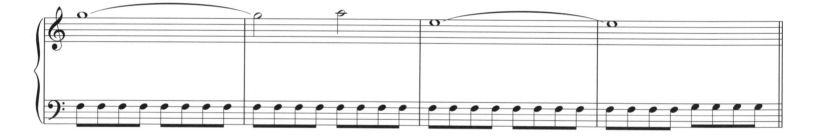

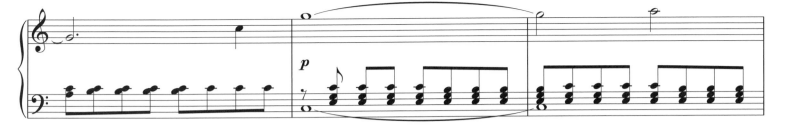

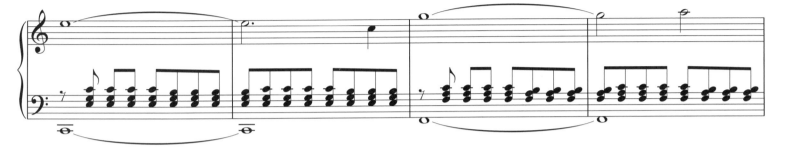

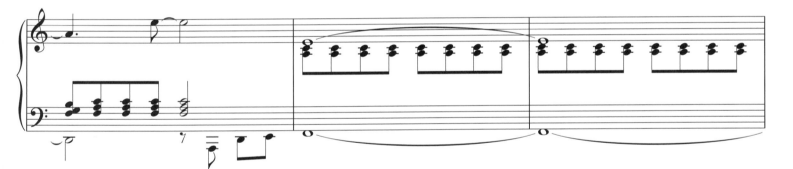

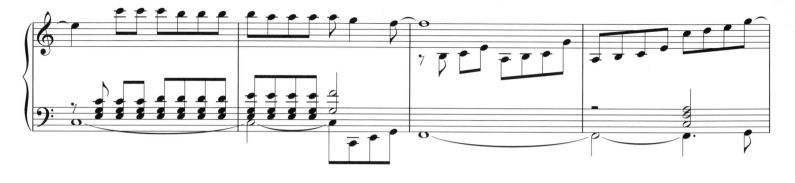

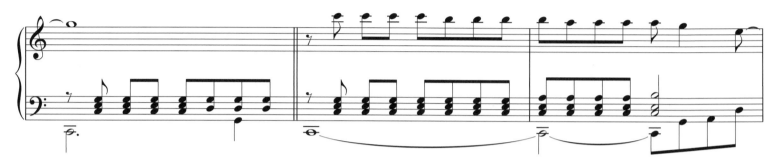

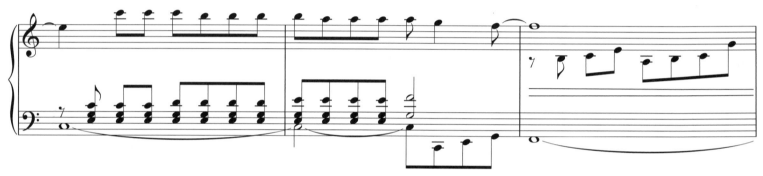